[AND TIME ERODES LIKE THUNDER]

ZOË LUH

ASSURE PRESS

Copyright © 2020 by Zoë Luh

All Rights Reserved. No part of this book may be performed, recorded, used or reproduced in any manner whatsoever without the written consent of the author and the permission of the publisher except in the case of brief quotations embodied in critical articles and review.

An imprint of Assure Press Publishing & Consulting, LLC

www.assurepress.org

Publisher's Note: Assure Press books may be purchased for educational, business, or sales promotional use. For information please visit the website.

[and time erodes like thunder] / Zoë Luh. — 1st ed.

ISBN-13: 978-1-7335897-4-1
Library of Congress Control Number: 2020936180
eISBN-978-1-7335897-5-8

PREFACE

content warning for sexual assault, death, and medical violence. please take care of yourself and be gentle.

CONTENTS

Home   1

[FALL]

I wake with tears longer than his hair	7
Ode to Disrespect	9
Tricube in si-lence	11
Trial of the Cannibal	12
Instead of doctoring viscera, I doctor the souls of others. -after Andy Sia	15

[WINTER]

WINTER IN AMBER

Dear Amber...	21
The beginning is always frozen...	22
I dream you are lying in a pool of blood...	24
I wish you were here...	25
Deep violet girl says...	26
Your dear friend Ruben died this week...	27
Tricube in mourning	29
explaining depression as something more than sadness	30
Clay	33
Dirge to seeds of blood	35

[SPRING]

the news article reads:	39
when he is not with me, he is still here: him and him and his hands.	42
i come from strong women and them from me	44
thyme	46
alternate universe in which right now i'm happy	48

,to feel safe after. It's really fucking hard to feel safe again.   50
Tricube in tsu-nami   51

[SUMMER]

fern   55
Elegy of Summer   56
grief is a gift   57
in late summer   58
Tricube in ten-der   59
re-examination   60

About the Author   63

[AND TIME ERODES LIKE THUNDER]

Home

comfort and this still feels like home to me
find home in tunnels under earth

trees without roots somehow still standing
and i find home in cavities

in that darkness and space in between
learn to hold my tongue

in anxious knots and tangles
i am learning to keep quiet again

i am learning to be bruised again
my tongue does not fit this half choked hand

and home twists through too-big teeth
this is not home anymore

where ghosts rise again through throat and breath and bruises

this is not home
...

maybe if i move out to the desert
live in air with so little water,

it won't drown my voice. i could move to desert
i always loved red rocks and

heat to bring you back home
to bones

i want to find home and
maybe if i find home in myself i

won't have to tie feet into one space
tell my heels they must grow roots.

i want to find home in myself again
want to find home

feet carry blisters where old roots
torn away are memory

and i don't have memories anymore
but still i find home in me.

i pull tangles and thorns from taste-buds
and spit ghosts into thousand-foot waterfalls, watch them fall
to mist

i bless my feet and bury toes in soft earth,
watch my legs grow swirls of grain and bark

place my palms to my roots
and ask for forgiveness

for too many bruised words.
i stretch leaves to the sky to sing, and

thank the mists and fire for amethyst roots
knowing i am home

i am forgiving
i am healing

I am making home for me

[FALL]

I wake with tears longer than his hair

he is still here with me
when he is not with me he is still here
him and him and his hands

I anticipate the day when the memory of him doesn't
climb into bed with me　　　comma
hold this moment open for me I need to　　　comma breathe
Haunt me like I am Already gone and I am gone again under your
comma　　　blankets and your　　　comma hair and maybe
if I add enough　　　,,,　　　here it will
give me enough　　　,　　　　space to , Breathe but I
can't　　,　　end this with a period because a period would enditforever

and I made a　　,　　promise
one night to never　　,　　endmyself again
I have that　,　　tattooed on my wrist it reminds me that
you will not　　,　　win but tonight　　　,　　I need somethingmore than the
Space I get from a　　,　　I need a   breath I need　　,
　　a semicolon
orsomethingmorelikeaperiod

last night I dreamt of comfort and
warmthSafe wrapped around me transparent cloth
a boy talks about how he wants to grow his hair out like vines
curly and soft in my fingers

will you hold this moment open for me
I want to stay here with Safe forever
I wonder about the day when the memory of him

Doesn't climb into bed with me cocooning
me like a comforter the memory of
him and him and his hands

holding me so close
your vines are coffin to me
I am wrapped so tight
I can't breathe   ,
I can't   breathe

I will not break under this weight I   Heavy
but I need a space to help me breathe again

Ode to Disrespect

I am learning to interact with anger in a way that is more than undoing
fold me origami cloth until
I learn to love
how my voice shakes and whistles
love the pain of draining away
gentle rain through tsunamis and tenderness and

when a boy shows up
all legs and puppy-smile and acid-filled dreams
walls curve into me
break and
swirl around
his smile tastes too bright
he says
"your face is getting lopsided"
as he twists into a question mark

well my face has kissed the sun,
cheekbones like Himalayas they rise above,
touch the sky, my face is angelic and my
feather-magenta lips don't hesitate when he says
my face is lopsided, so
I tell him I need a break

when a boy doesn't show up
I leave his shirt on a bench outside
note reads: I didn't wash it,
you can wash your stuff when you wash yourself,
like river,
clean of irresponsibility and

I am learning to use my anger
I am learning to love my anger
I am learning to fold my anger into careful hearts and
gift myself love notes –admirer not so secret-
boil chocolate into flowers
to eat like I eat your disrespect and

last year
I let a boy boil me rotten
remember how blood blooms on tissues like roses in spring
spring promises me
that I will never be treated that way again
spring tells me to gather my love for myself
save my anger too and
I spin thorns into rose petals.

I am learning respect.

I am learning to love and still respect myself
be soft, little bird
and let long-legged boys and blood-orange tissues wash away
like river
anger coil into me and back where they once stood,
I care for myself,
let my voice earthquake until it shakes free of
lies and
fear and
whispers of not enough and
let me be fire again
until I stand
like flowers cracking through ice
robed in anger and love

Tricube in si-lence

and i al-
ways breathe small,
quiet, and

never ask
for my needs
for air, and

now i de-
mand not world,
but enough

Trial of the Cannibal

All rise.
Department One of the Superior Court is now in session.
Judge Luh presiding.
Please be seated.
Calling the case of the Cannibal versus the Sudoku People. Are both sides ready?

Your Honor and people of the jury:
under the law my client is
presumed innocent until proven guilty
my client has been accused of the criminal action of
existing while disabled.
Defendant, please take the stand.

The evidence will show that I
was accused on the afternoon of
April 8th, 2019
of asking for housing accommodations that
actually fit my accessibility needs
in a meeting with the director of residential education
mid-sentence, neck open
fingers found around my hope
protecting hope
protecting safety
from your teeth,
cannibal
if you label Sudoku broken
what does that justify?

> a. I hereby find the medical industry guilty of abuse against disabled people.

    b. I hereby find those associated with the medical industry guilty.

    c. I hereby find those not providing access to disabled people perpetrators of violence against disabled people.

The Defense will now present the evidence.

1. The majority of students of color live on South Campus.

2. None of the buildings on South Campus have been renovated recently.

3. this school is hungry for people of color
   can't consume enough of our culture
   while you suck program funding out of our empty shell
   and leave our homes in disrepair

4. disabled people of color are set aside for later

   separated from our communities
   you swallow us there in the abyss

5. environmental pollutants dig wells in my body,
   this could dig me six feet under

6. schools do not have the resources to take care of their buildings and have environmental pollutants
   I've gone to schools that almost dug me under
   I've been kicked out of schools for death being burden

7. there used to be a hallway in the basement of my school they nicknamed death row
   for the number of people who were made sick,
   made death

meaning schools do not have the resources to support the
people they make
    un-able

8. there is a history of marginalized people not being believed
for their stories
and you tell me I do not have enough evidence
but I can tell you that I know my experience
I can tell you I know you lied to me in your meeting of
shadows
I can tell you that I know that you know this is unsafe
I can tell you every way these buildings in your arms
violate the Americans with Disabilities Act
and

9. this school wants me to live where it will dig me under
wants to consume my differences

10. those who do not provide access to disabled people are
    guilty of violence against
        disabled people

11. I hereby find you violent.
    I hereby find you predator.
    I hereby find you guilty.

    You are guilty.

The defense rests.

Judge, your ruling?

Instead of doctoring viscera, I doctor the souls of others. - after Andy Sia

Little bird,
I remember your
whirlpool eyes of the storm are gentle to me and
now I feel lost too
without your hurricanes, and
we still hold hands when we talk.

I say something feels off, and
I miss you
you tell me you don't know
you don't know
and I don't either
but I know what home feels like on the
roof of the jazz building
know spinning clay in my fingers will always feel like friendship
and granola doesn't taste the same before 2 am

You say I like to fix my friendships.
And I do.
Maybe that's too much,
But I don't want to give up before we fall away
Or fall afraid
And maybe that's the difference
Because you're afraid of feeling anything
And my nightmares are filled with feelings of nothing
Empty spaces between my
Ribcage and hollow spinal cord
Cerebrospinal fluid has no purpose, so drips aimlessly
Down
To rest on my stomach and
Wait

And maybe that whirlpool in my belly is the reason
I feel heavy when I see you,
or maybe I feel heavy because
I've never been good enough at science to become a doctor
And I don't know how to fix this
I don't know

[WINTER]

winter in Amber

"How are you?"

"Still shocked honestly"

"Me too. Maggie said it isn't looking good. It looks like she went in the river. She didn't sound good when she called…I think she might be dead"

"me too."

* * *

Dear Amber,

I am reading *Parable of the Sower* today and thinking of you. I'm struck by your capacity for love and kindness that most people can't begin to imagine. I remember sitting for tea with you last spring. We had work to do, but before that, you wanted to check in to see how I was doing after the recent shootings. I remember your surprise when I asked the same of you. Every person came before yourself. You gave your smile away in pieces, gifting a part of your soul to every community, every soul you met. The kindest thing you said to me was that I remind you of yourself. I can only hope to be like you, you're someone I admire more than anyone.

The police pulled your body from the river this morning. It's been months. They said there's no reason to suspect foul play. They said they suspect you took your own life.

I am afraid, chère amie. I have always been similar to you, and the river too has called to me softly. In my love for you, I am afraid.

You have the most beautiful soul.

* * *

The beginning is always frozen
    this year is

        melting
        so soon and
                like the river will become liquid, and
                maybe then you will be here again.

                I imagine when the ice begins to
                      t
                          r
                            i
                               c
                                  k
                                     l
                                         e
        into something less
        we will pull you from new water and
        you will be found

and lost

    again

when that happens I want to say
    I can't say I know your pain,
        but I know bruised ribs flow to thick breath
            pills pull dangerous intoxicated yearning
                to be something more
                or not at all
        I know when hope drips away.
            answer the phone, all I hear is
"I love you."

I wish you were here today. I'm still reading *Parable of the Sower* and thinking of you again. The ocean is beautiful, waves fold into me and the water goes on forever, ceasing to exist beyond the skyline. I remember you like I remember that water, so I guess it's fitting that's where you found your last moment. But water is also healing to me. I wish you were here right now. I think you would understand this feeling I have: not quite mourning, while appreciating the complete beauty.

But there is darkness here on these sands.

I can feel your energy in the wave and sand dunes. You mourn like the wave disappearing to beyond: rhythmic and full bodied. It is part of healing. We must cry to the ocean until it brings us home and healed.

Maybe that's why the river was your last place to heal in peace.

I'm feeling the breeze and the sun. They feel like you. I'm glad they finally found your body. I will hold your spirit and let tears bring peace and water.

* * *

Deep violet girl says I am the softest person she knows. We laugh and list-off our friends, trying to find someone with emotions water falling out of their head in strands longer than mine. They can't come close. If my hair were alive, she would be a silk boa constrictor, and wrap around your fears so gently. If my fear was alive, she would be a desert cactus with spikes bending into heat, holding water to feed dry throats. If my hunger was alive, she would pick every fruit from coconut trees, feed the milk to you, and catch your tears in the shells.

Amber, you are soft in the way I am. And you never ran away from that. You encouraged me and reminded me not to be ashamed of my emotions, they make me stronger. They make me more able to create community and kindness and change. My soft holds life like clouds ready for thunder, and I will pour down life to feed desert.

Amber, I heard in your last phone call you said you wanted to join eternity. And I will not forget you. You are soft sand, strong water.
I want to be ocean with you.

Amber,

Your dear friend Ruben died this week. I didn't know him well, but it hurts to see you again. I know they all mean well but it hurts to see the posts circling in spirals. We were just beginning to heal from, for, and with you. healing takes time and water and there is not enough.

I thank water for the life a picture can bring.

Rest in Peace and Power.

Tricube in mourning

if this is

mourning, then

i am half

buried in-

side myself

in quiet

i will mourn,

heal silent-

ly inside

explaining depression as something more than sadness

I want to say:

When I'm depressed I'm not sad

I want to say:

When I'm depressed I cry all the time

But I am not sad

I want to say:

When I'm depressed I cry all the time

And I'm not sad

But tears are the only way I feel anything

I want to say:

Depression is unwashed tea cups,

piles of clothes on the floor, and

blinds closed 3/4s of the way, because

I know I need light

but having my blinds all the way open and being able to see

reality is too much for me

Depression is separating medications into small bags,

no more than three pills in each...

hiding the bags in different boxes so they're harder to reach

Depression is giving all my medications to someone I trust

Depression is breaking my scissors,

leaving my knife in the shared kitchen,

going back and hiding the knife in the shared kitchen,

throwing away the parts of my scissors

Depression is made up of lists,

names,

phone numbers,

1

2

3

steps before calling, but

always calling anyways

I want to say:

Depression is saving notes like lifelines,

a portable jar full of love I can't feel

Depression is writing myself love notes and

at night writing every positive thing from that day

Depression is feeling like my love notes aren't real

I want to say:

I don't understand depression.

I don't understand depression, but I understand reflection,

I understand survival techniques as water

I understand water and numbness

I understand earth, and the way my ancestors are dirt again

so earth is in my bones, so I am made of clay,

so I will make it, until I don't have to think about

making it,

or water,

or scissors

Clay

Depression is a looking glass,   if the mirror was   bent
at   angles, colored deep indigo   and
                                              cracked
then glued together again.
    Or maybe it's the curse of Narcissus in reverse.
    When I look in the mirror it only shows monster,
    only shows shattered,
    only shares shadow.
I stare anyways,   pick at my skin   until I peel away layers,
    reveal newborn clay, and
        shape her into someone the mirror adores.

And I always loved clay.

Earth is so pliable.
    She is the giver of life to un-seeable organisms,
    to plants,
    to flowers,
    to me.
Earth is pliable and soft,
    but clay is the   in-between,   standing somewhere
            closer to rock.
Clay is made up of   fine particles, and the delicate particles
growtogether, determined not to allow anything to permeate her
body.
Instead,
    clay holds water,   doesn't let it fall through.
It is difficult for plants to grow in clay,
        but she has healing nutrients.
            Her nutrients are the   givers of life.
Cultures used to use clay as medicine,
        understood the magic in earth's particles,

>   how the giver of life restores.
>   In Chinese medicine,
>   they used to eat the clay to heal their pains,
>   hope that she would heal our bodies,
>   heal our souls,
>   hope for more life

And I guess that's what I want.

I want to be clay and to   hold clay,
      have her heal my arms,
      my skin,
      my mirror.
And maybe if I go back to my roots,
      honor my ancestors and eat their bones of clay,

I could be healed…I will forgive like clay…I will be earth again

Dirge to seeds of blood

feel my seed grow small
i mourn the child i will never have.

i never regret this illness my body breeds
but i mourn again
knowing i am not less woman
        not less giver
        not less mother or care
i know i have life inside my veins   not belly

and i always said i didn't want children,
and maybe i don't,

but empty blooms inside me and
there is sorrow here
when i bleed, i bleed more woman than plasma

and
in Chinese culture, to bear a child is the
core of femininity
        it is duty
        it is creation of community itself
and though my family is not traditional
and i have always said i didn't want children
i mourn and

mourn again
knowing that with my illness
blooms miscarriages, water of life slipping from me
and my culture
      my culture
will never see me as woman
will never see me whole

[SPRING]

the news article reads:

The 17-year-old accused of stabbing his friend and
leaving her for dead
in the woods in Reynoldsburg, Ohio
was charged yesterday with
raping and kidnapping
her.

today I feel myself dripping through the bottom of a net
made from newspaper clippings,
unwashed pain,
washed-out colors
and maybe
if I build a glass jar,
fill it with all the colors I love
maybe
I will feel full again

today, dark violet girl tells me
she wasn't allowed to go to that park
jagged rocks aren't as dangerous as nice guys and
for my first date, my ex took me to Pine Quarry Park
I remember almost falling
down
the rocky ravine
remember hands catching me mid-air
and
I remember when I was a child
I loved catching butterflies.
loved holding transient rainbows in my net

today I feel myself dripping
dripping

through the net
my colors are washed
translucent

the news article reads:
Tinder date leads to murder charges.

I delete Tinder off my phone
stop answering texts
I finally block his number and
I swipe left on every man I see
tired of being white enough for them to swallow but
exotic enough to fulfill their fantasies and
one time my ex called me his Chinese Princess,
trapped me under his holographic net,
they always want to trap women of color between their palms
colors too bright not to be caught

and I still can't tell if he was kidding
but it doesn't matter because
he is just one nice guy and
there are enough nice guys for all of us and
there are too many nice guys and
fuck them all anyway
I have too many articles on my timeline
the headlines read --
the reporter says --
the newspapers and blurred words and paragraphs and –
I'm falling again
through the net

and

I remember when I was younger,

a woman told me that
butterflies have a chemical in their wings
that makes them poisonous to those who eat them;
the brighter the colors, the more dangerous

and I promise I will only wear scarlet,
azure blue,
and pink for you,
if you swallow any part of me I will paint you burnt magenta
because
my glass jar is full,
mouth too full with breaking news and
when these men eat us
we poison back
and they eat anyways
and they eat
and I will poison
butterfly
colors too bright for you to wash away

when he is not with me, he is still here: him and him and his hands.

I anticipate the day when the memory of him doesn't
climb into bed with me   comma
Hold this moment open for me I need to   comma   breath   comma
Haunt me like I am Already gone and I am gone again under your
comma   blankets and your   comma   hair and maybe
if I add enough   ,,,   here it will
give me enough   ,   space to   ,   Breathe

and

Last night I dreamt of comfort and
warmth   Safe wrapped around me like transparent cloth,
hold this moment gently for me,
I want to stay here with safe forever.

I am safe
forever
in me

I will not break under this weight I   Heavy
and I need a space to help me breathe again

Breathe

I can't say I know your pain
but I know pain.
Take my hand and I can heal with you
I have healed already

let our hands both be water,
gentle rain through tsunamis, we hold water tender

we are tender

i come from strong women and them from me

in 1956 a girl named Molly Daly disappeared to Fairview Hospital and Training Center. She was two years old. in 1959 Fairview released a video showing their care. they show nurses and a cafeteria. they don't show handcuffs, acid baths, sexual assault and torture that was everyday life. Molly stayed at Fairview for three and a half decades.

my great grandmother was
diagnosed with schizophrenia
and was charged to a mental
hospital
and given shock treatment
every day
until she lost her mind between
waves of electricity.
shock therapy is still legal
in the U.S.
and i feel her pain in lines
    between
legislation

my grandmother was a
double amputee
when she fell ill with a minor illness
she went to the hospital for medicine
and never came out
after careless hands slipped treatments
and ivs were switched to drip
drip
her life gone, and
disabled people die at the hands of
care
we die and they say they
cared

i am 20 years old
and have held the hand of death
spent more time in hospitals
than high school
i know how to negotiate with doctors
know my school will never protect me
unless i
demand
and i do demand
    for myself and my mothers before me

because
i know the feel of dirt under fingernails
    from my ancestors' graves
i know dirt in our lungs and
we sing
so loudly they can't ignore
must pay homage to the graves
that bear our stories
kneel to the earth and
ask not for forgiveness
but love

understand we hurt at their
hands
die at their needles
and still they say they can't see our bones

and wash blood from their
needles and knives

my mother lived 30 years
before being diagnosed with the
disease
she and i call home
and they say they care
say they are healing

and i ask you to sing with us,
    anger with us
    love with us
        and our ancestors
        from the ground

forgiveness isn't enough
but we give it freely,
we give it painfully

feel our love radiate from 6 feet under
and in the end i forgive
and i love and hurt
and am stronger

thyme

today i didn't get out of bed until 12:23
in a Tuesday morning kind of way
when i don't want to remember
every Tuesday morning in the crumbling church parking lot
clarinet hands take too much from me

today my therapist tells me it takes most survivors a minimum of two years
to peel away their quiet
and i wonder why the words were so eager to escape mine

i wonder if practice makes the consonants easier to swallow
if my mother's tongue carries the same words as mine,
make grooves in between my taste-buds, does that ready the words
to fall through my tongue?

i read that one in three women, and because I am one
does this mean my sisters are safe now?
i wonder if one day I'll be less afraid,
i might have a daughter.
what tunnels will she have
wonder if i have carved her hollow before she is even a thought

today i write apology under every breath
every thank you and i love you
i am so sorry

carry my hurt too and I do not want to
lower this grief into the grasses,
wishing for a word softer than acceptance
apologizing the way down

today it's raining.
morning is filled with clouds
all puffy eyes from crying
you can't see the sun
only rain freckles on pavement
i know the rain gives life to the earth

and today i bend to my ancestors,
touch the earth and know I am touching their bones.
i ask for forgiveness
for not understanding their pain
and when the rain falls it falls as golden light
and the grasses grow soft again.

i touch my throat and ask myself for forgiveness
for ever blaming myself
for every anger, every pain
i lift my face
and when my tears fall, they fall golden rain
and my smile grows soft again

alternate universe in which right now i'm happy

in this universe secondary succession doesn't have to come after the fire
and when we grow, we grow flowers 7-feet-tall
and our petals give shade to our fears,
cradles them and gives them shelter to heal
like we have healed
softly and surrounded by grasses and light

in this universe there is no such thing as loneliness
not because we are never alone
but because when we are
it feels like coming home

in this universe there is no such thing as guilt
because we forgive ourselves for mistakes
and there is no such thing as shame
because we know no mistake defines who we are
we know that no pain can degrade our worth

in this universe there are no such things as flashbacks
because there are no nights we need to avoid remembering
there is no poison ivy hiding in the grasses
and we don't need to make lists of people to call when we aren't okay
because we are already okay here

in this universe there is no such thing as a crisis plan
because life always feels worth it
and the only thing at 4 am is peace
and the sound of dreams spinning through straw

in this universe we don't have to say

"I'm trying to forgive you"
because there is nothing to forgive
and we don't have to say
"I love you but this hurts too much"
because here love is never painful

and in this universe we are not afraid to love
and we are not afraid of ourselves
in this universe we cry when we are sad and our tears water the
ground beneath our
        fears
and instead of drowning
they sprout into mushrooms
and we eat our fears sprinkled with paprika and hope
and we are okay

in this universe we are not afraid to love ourselves
and in this universe we are still innocent
and in this universe we are not afraid
and when we are afraid
there is no fire to burn it all away
so we gather our fears into bouquets
and propagate them to plant between our toes
and we watch them grow and give life to insects and animals
and those little animals find shelter in our shadow
we provide home

in this universe I am home

in this universe I have found home in myself
and not someone or somewhere else
and I am not afraid to be happy again

,to feel safe after. It's really fucking hard to feel safe again.

upside-down midnight turns words into flowers
into confessions
i tell him
i have held the stars in his soul
beautiful like the night is soft

i feel comfort in upside-down night skies
safe in velvet arms
and I didn't know I could feel safe like that again
didn't think I could feel safe again
but stars warm my skin and
feather lips
wrap me in cloth and whisper your universe
soft star
stay here until morning covers

Tricube in tsu-nami

and in the
end healing
is soft rain

gentle tsu-
nami breath
quiet strength

and forgive-
ness, tender
golden love

[SUMMER]

fern

this sad fern/heavy with my
sorrow
      sorrow
           sorrow
      i love a boy whose hands fall heavy on his head
                                              and
    guilt can be more corrosive than
                acid
    i love myself and my head falls heavy on my hands
        more metal than water
        i am strong in forgiveness
                forgiveness
                    forgiveness
      is a tool
        a gift i love i love
    strength in softness
        of leaves and moss
      soft wind on a cloudy day
sad fern heavy with grief
    you grow in half-shade
    form from dirt and decay
i love

Elegy of Summer

in spring we grow sad/soft/summer/is for healing/and heavy hands/heavy heads/tired of feeling/believing this will get better/grief/holds our hands/reminds us we are like seasons/temporary/beautiful/harsh/hands hold waterfalls/reminds me to feel/ reminds me that knives to do belong on skin/in summer i grow sad/sad/soft/tender/summer is for learning strength/is for learning grief/is for seasons

grief is a gift/and i am grieving/my love his guilt/
and his hands fall heavy on his head
i love a boy/and we hurt too/my love/
my love/my/love/i/too/grieve/lost time/and hope/
i want to roll back time on a stretcher and
pluck each pain from it's place,
instead i give kisses and
heal a wound that never existed
i want to fold my love in my wings
roll back the roof of his head and
pluck each pain from it's place
instead give love and comfort
i want to stretch myself
into unknown future and
plant tenderness as seed
watch it grow to love and forgiveness
grief is a gift and
i am grieving
my pain a waterfall and ocean
my fain gives life to tenderness
tides recede
and let seeds grow in their wake
and we flood again
and we grow
tender

in late summer/the grass has started to/turn/return/to decay and start new/i am grass/slowly turning/returning to myself/to start again/i love a boy/and even when it is sad/this love is soft/my love/take/my hands/wrap love around us/i love/i love/i love/even when I am sad/even as i/grow brittle/from the sun/in this summer/we are soft

Tricube in ten-der

i find home,
myself, in
safety and

i breathe soft
i love ten-
der, gentle

let love breathe
and me too
in my home

re-examination

the Americans with Disabilities Act says that
places of work
and institutions of education
must provide "reasonable accommodations" for disabled people.
but what happens
when we don't fit your idea of reasonable?

every
     re
          re
               re-examination of sepia traumas
in half-choked classrooms and offices
and
if you label me broken
what does that justify?
If I label myself broken
What does that justify?

we should not live in the twilight
in between care and undefined fear
tell me:
am I supposed to feel safe here?

you ask me
to justify my existence
say I am too much water not enough sand
so I pull your words out into clouds of dust
you ask me how I dare demand to be safe
and my mouth forms a tornado to blow your words to the stars
you ask how I can think I am ever enough
and I say

I am vast and larger than any forest
I wish I could stretch out my arms
embrace the trees as they hold me
and
I don't know what clouds taste like but
I scoop the light into my mouth, and it doesn't taste like water or air,
it tastes like fresh stardust and honeyed waves
and in that I know I will be okay
I taste the sky and know I am
more than flesh and mistakes and crisscrossed genetics

I will scoop the clouds into my mouth
eat every light in the sky and
from the atmosphere rain onto earth.
from my tongue the grasses reverse their destruction and
forests grow from my breath

every twinkling houselight becomes a star and
floats out of the grasses
and we are all okay again.
We are healing and
we hold out our hands and sing

ABOUT THE AUTHOR

Zoë Luh lives in Columbus, Ohio and is a Gemini sun and moon, and a Scorpio rising. She is a Comparative American Studies major at Oberlin College, and writes and performs poems as a member of their poetry team, OSLAM. Her writing crosses the intersections of disability, race and gender with the complexities of healing and joy. Several of her articles on racial ableism appear in the *Oberlin Review*.

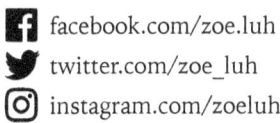

facebook.com/zoe.luh
twitter.com/zoe_luh
instagram.com/zoeluh

www.ingramcontent.com/pod-product-compliance
Lightning Source LLC
Chambersburg PA
CBHW021131080526
44587CB00012B/1238